P9-BXW-947

Bananas
Pineapples
Grapes
Berries
Melons
Bananas

**PLANTS
WE EAT**

Pineapples
Grapes
Berries
Melons
Bananas
Pineapples
Grapes
Berries
Melons
Bananas
Pineapples
Grapes
Berries

Yes, We Have Bananas

Fruits from Shrubs & Vines

Meredith Sayles Hughes

Lerner Publications Company/Minneapolis

Check out the author's website at www.foodmuseum.com/hughes

Lerner Publications Company
A Division of the Lerner Publishing Group
241 First Avenue North
Minneapolis, MN 55401

Website address: www.lernerbooks.com

Designer: Steven P. Foley
Assistant Designer: Réna Dehler
Editor: Amy M. Boland
Photo Researcher: Beth Osthoff

LIBRARY OF CONGRESS CATALOGING-IN-PUBLICATION DATA

Hughes, Meredith Sayles.
    Yes, we have bananas: fruits from shrubs & vines / Meredith Sayles Hughes.
        p. cm. – (Plants we eat)
    Includes index.
    Summary: Describes the historical origins, domestication, uses, growing requirements, harvesting, and shipping of bananas, pineapples, berries, grapes, and melons.
    ISBN 0–8225–2836–3 (lib. bdg. : alk. paper)
    1. Fruit—Juvenile literature. 2. Fruit-culture—Juvenile literature. [1. Fruits. 2. Fruit culture.] I. Title.
II. Series: Hughes, Meredith Sayles. Plants we eat.
SB457.2.H84 2000
634—dc21   98–45738

Manufactured in the United States of America.
1 2 3 4 5 6 – JR – 05 04 03 02 01 00

The glossary on page 77 gives definitions of words shown in **bold type** in the text.

Contents

Introduction

Plants make all life on our planet possible. They provide the oxygen we breathe and the food we eat. Think about a burger and fries. The meat comes from cattle, which eat plants. The fries are potatoes cooked in oil from soybeans, corn, or sunflowers. The burger bun is a wheat product. Ketchup is a mixture of tomatoes, herbs, and corn syrup or the sugar from sugarcane. How about some onions or pickle relish with your burger?

How Plants Make Food

By snatching sunlight, water, and carbon dioxide from the atmosphere and mixing them together—a complex process called **photosynthesis**—green plants create food energy. The raw food energy is called glucose, a simple form of sugar. From this storehouse of glucose, each plant produces fats, carbohydrates, and proteins—the elements that make up the bulk of the foods humans and animals eat.

Sunlight peeks through the branches of a plant-covered tree in a tropical rain forest, where all the elements exist for photosynthesis to take place.

First we eat, then we do everything else.

—M. F. K. Fisher

Plants offer more than just food. They provide the raw materials for making the clothes you're wearing and the paper in books, magazines, and newspapers. Much of what's in your home comes from plants—the furniture, the wallpaper, and even the glue that holds the paper on the wall. Eons ago plants created the gas and oil we put in our cars, buses, and airplanes. Plants even give us the gum we chew.

On the Move

Although we don't think of plants as beings on the move, they have always been pioneers. From their beginnings as algaelike creatures in the sea to their movement onto dry land about 400 million years ago, plants have colonized new territories. Alone on the barren rock of the earliest earth, plants slowly established an environment so rich with food, shelter, and oxygen that some forms of marine life took up residence on dry land. Helped along by birds who scattered seeds far and wide, plants later sped up their travels, moving to cover most of our planet.

Early in human history, when few people lived on the earth, gathering food was everyone's main activity. Small family groups were nomadic, venturing into areas that offered a source of water, shelter, and foods such as fruits, nuts, seeds, and small game animals. After they had eaten up the region's food sources, the family group moved on to another spot. Only when people noticed that food plants were renewable—that the berry bushes would bear fruit again and that grasses gave forth seeds year after year—did family groups begin to settle in any one area for more than a single season.

Organisms that behave like algae—small, rootless plants that live in water

It's a Fact!

The term *photosynthesis* comes from Greek words meaning "putting together with light." This chemical process, which takes place in a plant's leaves, is part of the natural cycle that balances the earth's store of carbon dioxide and oxygen.

Native Americans were the first peoples to plant crops in the Americas.

Domestication of plants probably began as an accident. Seeds from a wild plant eaten at dinner were tossed onto a trash pile. Later a plant grew there, was eaten, and its seeds were tossed onto the pile. The cycle continued on its own until someone noticed the pattern and repeated it deliberately. Agriculture radically changed human life. From relatively small plots of land, more people could be fed over time, and fewer people were required to hunt and gather food. Diets shifted from a broad range of wild foods to a more limited but more consistent menu built around one main crop such as wheat, corn, cassava, rice, or potatoes. With a stable food supply, the world's population increased and communities grew larger. People had more time on their hands, so they turned to refining their skills at making tools and shelter and to developing writing, pottery, and other crafts.

Plants We Eat

This series examines the wide range of plants people around the world have chosen to eat. You will discover where plants came from, how they were first grown, how they traveled from their original homes, and where they have become important and why. Along the way, each book looks at the impact of certain plants on society and discusses the ways in which these food plants are sown, harvested, processed, and sold. You will also discover that some plants are key characters in exciting high-tech stories. And there are plenty of opportunities to test recipes and to dig into other hands-on activities.

The series Plants We Eat divides food plants into a variety of informal categories. Some plants are prized for their seeds, others for their fruits, and some for their underground roots, tubers, or bulbs. Many plants offer leaves or stalks for good eating. Humans convert some plants into oils and others into beverages or flavorings. The part of a plant that develops from a flower and contains the plant's seeds is called a fruit. Fruit's role in nature is to ensure that new plants will grow from the old. Many fruits also provide flavorful nourishment for people and animals. *Yes, We Have Bananas: Fruits from Shrubs & Vines* presents a cornucopia of fruits with one thing in common: none of them grow on trees. Two fruits, the banana and the pineapple, grow in the **tropics,** and both are available around the world thanks to high-tech, high-speed production and delivery techniques. Although it can grow as tall as a tree, the bright banana is actually a giant **herb** with a soft rather than a woody stem. Also considered an herb, the sweet and juicy pineapple emerges from a low, thorny growth resembling a cactus.

Grapes grow on climbing vines. **Berries,** everyone's favorite eat-them-straight-from-the-hand fruit, typically grow low on small plants or shrubs in cooler parts of the world. A true berry is a single, enlarged ovary (the part of a flower that becomes a fruit) with many seeds embedded in its flesh. But generally people will call any small, seedy fruit a berry. Viny melons grow along the ground in dry, warm places, giving hot-weather refreshment to all.

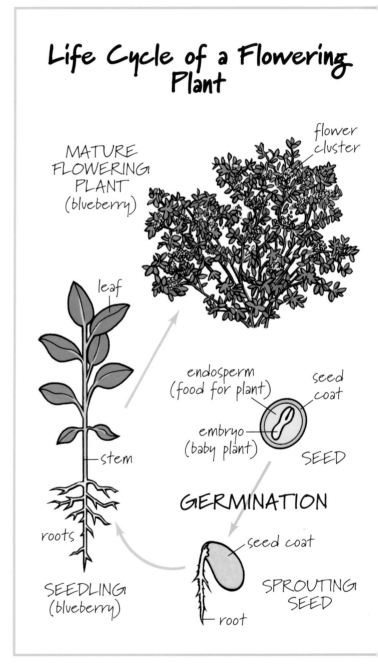

Life Cycle of a Flowering Plant

flower cluster

MATURE FLOWERING PLANT (blueberry)

leaf

endosperm (food for plant)

seed coat

embryo (baby plant)

SEED

stem

GERMINATION

seed coat

roots

SPROUTING SEED

SEEDLING (blueberry)

root

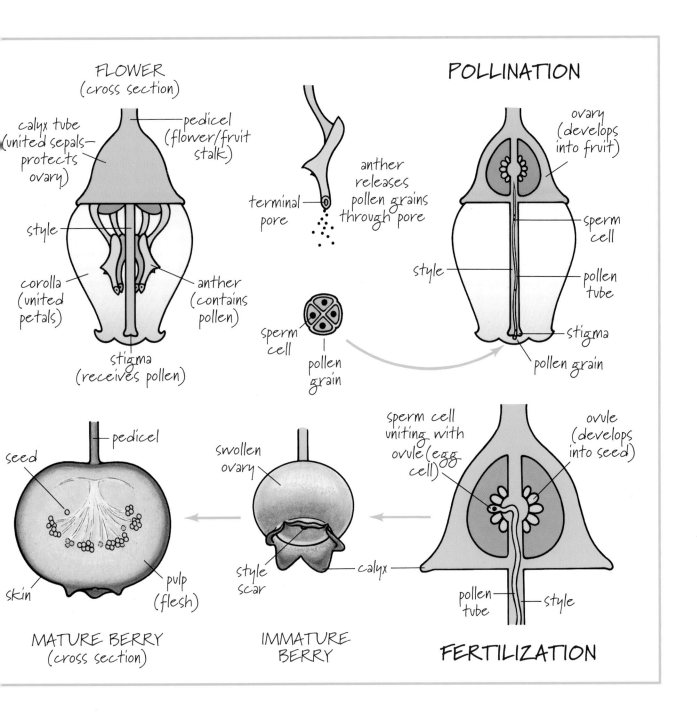

FLOWER
(cross section)

calyx tube
(united sepals—
protects
ovary)

pedicel
(flower/fruit
stalk)

style

corolla
(united
petals)

anther
(contains
pollen)

stigma
(receives pollen)

terminal
pore

anther
releases
pollen grains
through pore

sperm
cell

pollen
grain

POLLINATION

ovary
(develops
into fruit)

sperm
cell

style

pollen
tube

stigma

pollen grain

seed

pedicel

skin

pulp
(flesh)

MATURE BERRY
(cross section)

swollen
ovary

style
scar

calyx

IMMATURE
BERRY

sperm cell
uniting with
ovule (egg
cell)

ovule
(develops
into seed)

pollen
tube

style

FERTILIZATION

Bananas
[*Musa sapientum*]

The tropical banana is one of the tallest herbs you'll ever see, sometimes growing as high as 40 feet. The plant grows from a **rhizome,** or thick underground stem, that produces shoots. Because it has no woody structure, the banana is not a tree, tall though it may be. The banana features some of the largest leaves among all plants, some growing as big as 12 feet long by 2 feet wide. The curved fruit grows on a long stalk and is picked green. Bananas turn their familiar yellow color at the marketplace or on kitchen counters throughout the world.

A box of ripe Costa Rican bananas is ready for shipment to market.

Here lies the body of our
Anna
Done to death by a
banana
It wasn't the fruit
That laid her low
But the skin of the thing
That made her go.

—Tombstone inscription,
Enosburg, Vermont

Thousands of years ago, the banana grew wild in the tropics of Southeast Asia, possibly in present-day Malaysia. The banana may even have had a huge homeland stretching from India to New Guinea, an island north of Australia.

The wild banana was hard and full of seeds, as are wild bananas today. Some early farmer must have seen promise in the tough fruit and selected the least seeded specimen for future propagation. Over time the resulting seedless, sweet, domesticated banana became a tropical staple.

Banana Travels

Little is known of the plant's earliest travels from its home base. In Southwest Asia, 7,000-year-old wall

Family Matters

To keep things straight in the huge families of plants and animals, scientists classify and name living things by grouping them according to shared features within each of seven major categories. The categories are kingdom, division or phylum, class, order, family, genus, and species. Species share the most features in common, while members of a kingdom or division share far fewer traits. This system of scientific classification and naming is called taxonomy. Scientists refer to plants and animals by a two-part Latin or Greek term made up of the genus and the species name. The genus name comes first, followed by the species name. When talking about a genus that has more than one commonly cultivated species, such as *Fragaria* (strawberries), we'll use only the genus name in the chapter heading. In the discussions about specific fruits, we'll list the two-part species name. Look at the banana's taxonomic name on page 10. Can you figure out to what genus the banana belongs? And to what species?

inscriptions left by the ancient people called Assyrians seem to depict the domesticated banana, but scholars are still undecided. Excavations in the valley of India's namesake river, the Indus, indicate that bananas were being cultivated 6,000 years ago. About 2,500 years ago, artisans at Ajanta, a south central Indian village remarkable for its ancient caves and temples, honored the banana in wall paintings. Around the same time, in 450 B.C., the banana made its first literary appearance in a Hindu holy book called the Ramayana. The book tells the tale of King Rama, considered to be the reincarnation of the Hindu god Vishnu. A famed slayer of dragons and monsters, Rama survived on the yellow fruit when no other food was available to him. Because the Hindus exalted Rama as a god, they revered the banana, too.

Somewhat later, in 327 B.C., the Greek historian Megasthenes accompanied a Greek invasion of India. He noted banana plants growing in the Indus Valley and wrote, "The plants bear fruit in a bunch." Even though the Greek soldiers saw and perhaps ate the banana, they didn't bring it home to plant—probably because it was too perishable to keep alive hundreds of miles from its orgins.

Arab traders doing business in India most likely brought the banana to the Arabian Peninsula, Egypt, and surrounding areas. Mocha, an ancient Arab port city in Yemen,

The wall paintings at Ajanta, India, depict the people and gods of ancient times.

was at one time a banana center. A garbled version of the city's name even gave the fruit its Latin name, *musa*. By the A.D. 600s, the Koran—the holy book of Islam, the main Arab religion—depicted the banana as the forbidden fruit in the Garden of Paradise.

Sometime around the 600s, Arabs took the banana plant on slave-trading journeys to East Africa. Perhaps Africans fleeing the slave traders carried banana plants into the interior of Africa. Some historians think that Indonesians, not Arabs, may have brought the plant to the African island of Madagascar, and the locals may have spread the plant throughout the continent from there.

As well as bringing bananas to Cordova, Spain, the Moors built this tower in the city. Bananas can make it in semitropical areas such as southern Spain but are most healthy in the true tropics.

When the North African Arabs known as Moors occupied Spain from the 700s to the 1200s, they established bananas in several Spanish cities. A scribe from Cordova, Spain, described the exotic fruit growing with olive and orange trees. Most of the Moorish banana plantings died out with the Moors' loss of political power. By the late 1490s, when Queen Isabella of Spain ordered the last of the Moors out of the country, Europeans in the area were no longer familiar with the banana.

Throughout the 1400s, Portuguese explorers sailed along Africa's western coast all the way to the Cape of Good Hope. Arriving on the central coast of West Africa in 1482, the Portuguese saw bananas as brand-new oddities. They invented the name *banana* for the plant, jumbling together different words from African dialects—among them *bana, gbana, funana,* and *abana.*

Bananas Go to America

Bananas finally made the leap to the Americas in 1516. A Spanish priest named Friar Tomás de Berlanga carried the plants with him from the Canary Islands, off Africa's Atlantic coast, to the Caribbean island of Hispaniola, which

Haiti and the Dominican Republic came to share. Friar Tomás was intent on converting the islanders to Christianity, not to banana culture. Nonetheless the banana caught on. Within a few years, the fruit was growing in Mexico and in many parts of Central America, reaching as far into South America as Peru.

Extremely wealthy Europeans imported bananas from the Caribbean. Legend has it that in the early 1800s, Josephine, first wife of the French emperor Napoleon Bonaparte, asked her mother to ship some bananas to Paris from the Caribbean island of Martinique. Did the bananas arrive in France dark brown and squishy? Did Napoleon try them or toss them in the trash? Napoleon was later exiled to the island of St. Helena, far off the western coast of Africa. There he again encountered bananas, this time as fritters sweetened with honey.

It's a Fact!

Some historians think that seagoing traders from the Pacific Islands may have brought banana plants to Peru one or two centuries before Friar Tomás arrived on Hispanola.

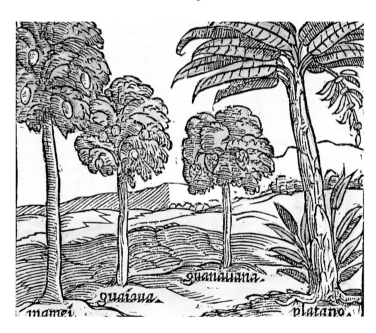

This European drawing of tropical Brazilian plants includes bananas, which are native to Asia.

Bananas Make the Big Time

For hundreds of years, the banana remained a curiosity—a luxury, even—to people who did not live in banana-growing countries. The North American banana boom began with a New England sea captain named Lorenzo Baker. In May 1870, Baker bought bananas on the Caribbean island of Jamaica. Eleven days later, he docked in Jersey City, New Jersey, where a grocer gave Baker top dollar for the desirable fruit. Convinced that bananas were the future, Baker went back to Jamaica, bought an entire shipload of bananas, and returned the following year to Boston. He sold the fruit to a produce merchant named Andrew Preston, and soon Baker was bringing Preston as many bananas as his ships could carry. By 1885 Baker was regularly shipping bananas from Jamaica to Boston on his own steamships, which made the trip in 10 to 12 days. Preston, sensing a golden opportunity for profits, joined forces with other buyers to create the Boston Fruit Company in that year.

Meanwhile, a New Yorker named Minor Keith ventured to the Central American country of Costa Rica to build a railroad. Keith planted bananas along the railroad so that the crop could be the new venture's first load of freight. Trains took the bananas to the east coast seaport of Limón, and then workers loaded them on ships bound for the United States. Keith found his initial banana customers in New Orleans, Louisiana, and in Mobile, Alabama. Bananas traveled from these coastal cities up the Mississippi River on steam paddle wheelers and across the United States by rail.

Plantains?

Yes, they are bananas, just a slightly different type. Plantains are larger than yellow bananas and are black when fully ripe. What's more, they must be cooked before eating. A staple of the West Indies (a large chain of islands in the eastern Caribbean Sea), plantains can be fried, baked, or mashed—in fact, treated much like a potato.

Just in from Costa Rica, a United Fruit Company banana boat docks at New Orleans around 1910.

Keith soon discovered the risks of the banana business. Hurricanes and diseases could strike the plantations and the workers, but the main problem was coordinating transportation. Planters, shippers, and marketers all worked independently. This meant that sometimes there were too many bananas for the ships available, and sometimes there were too few. Sometimes the bananas waited so long for a ship that they had rotted by the time they reached their destination.

Keith and others realized the need for cooperation to make their banana venture successful over the long term. In 1899 he and the Boston Fruit Company merged to form the United Fruit Company (UFC). Growing and selling soon were all under the control of one business.

The new corporation expanded its rail lines and banana plantations in Costa Rica. UFC's influence helped to make Costa Rica the first "banana republic." This pattern was repeated in other Central and South American countries such as Ecuador, Honduras, Paraguay, Panama, Guatemala, and Colombia.

The term "banana republic" is an unfavorable reference to a small, tropical country whose economy depends largely on one foreign-controlled export crop—in many cases, bananas.

Dancing Bananas

During the 1930s, Brazilian film star Carmen Miranda was the highest-paid female entertainer in the United States. Miranda made bananas part of her act—they waggled from her elaborate tropical headdresses. She was the inspiration for the cartoon songstress Chiquita Banana, who first appeared just after World War II (1939–1945) and ultimately became the logo of Chiquita Brands.

Banana plantations in these countries were created in swampy lowlands where few people lived. UFC had to bring workers in from the highlands, and soon company towns sprang up. By 1930 UFC was the largest employer in Central America. Critics often found fault with the firm for its large size and for its involvement in the finances of many Central American nations. But to its credit, the company paid its workers relatively well and provided them with housing, stores, medical care, and schooling.

UFC used technology to get bananas to market in good time. When the bananas were picked, ships with steam engines sped bananas to port faster than sailing ships could, and refrigerated ships kept the produce from ripening too soon. As a further precaution against the heat, banana boats were painted white to repel the sun's rays. People called the array of ships the Great White Fleet.

Communication systems also helped the bananas reach their market. Banana boats were the first in American tropical waters to be equipped with radios. With radio, growers, shippers, and buyers could communicate with one another about availability, demand, and timing of delivery. Improved communication prevented the arrival of too many ships at a single port, which could mean a glut of cheap bananas one week and a total absence of the fruit the next week.

In 1998 Tropical Storm Mitch hit Honduras hard. Unlike most such storms, which typically blow over quickly, Mitch became trapped in the country's lowlands and devastated the banana crop. The storm left the country's highways, railroads, and bridges in a shambles, too. Fruit companies in the area lost hundreds of millions of dollars and were forced to lay off thousands of workers. Growers can't replant their crop until Honduras can fix its transportation networks. It may take three years to bring the country's banana industry back up to speed.

A laid-off banana worker surveys Hurricane Mitch's aftermath at this ruined Chiquita Brands plantation in Honduras.

As the banana flower bud opens, the hands of young fruit appear.

Growing Bananas

Much of the work of banana farming is done by hand. In the spring, banana growers create new plantations out of tropical rain forest lands by felling trees and hacking away vines. Workers plant portions of banana rhizomes about 11 feet apart in the humid soil. After three months, the young plants emerge from the remaining undergrowth, which farmhands clear away to enable sun and rain to reach the ground. Because the banana isn't a tree, it has no branches. Instead it sends up one flowering stalk per plant, along with several smaller, secondary stalks. The primary shoot grows rapidly, as much as an inch a day. But the stalks are weak and can easily crack or fall down in even moderate wind. For this reason, the plants are sometimes tied to bamboo stakes.

After nine months of growth, the primary shoot produces a bud from the center. As the bud develops and opens, groups of tiny flowers appear, and each flower turns into a banana. The entire stem comprises about 150 bananas, or "fingers," clustered into seven or eight "hands"—that is, bunches that developed from the same group of flowers. A stem of bananas can weigh 85 pounds or more.

After harvest growers cut down the main shoot. Then they choose one of the secondary shoots they have been nurturing off the same rhizome and cut back the others. The remaining shoot becomes a new primary shoot. With care the same banana rhizome can produce a stem of fruit about every 10 months for a few years. Commercial banana plantations last for 10 to 20 years. After that time, the soil is ruined, and growers must clear a new tract of land.

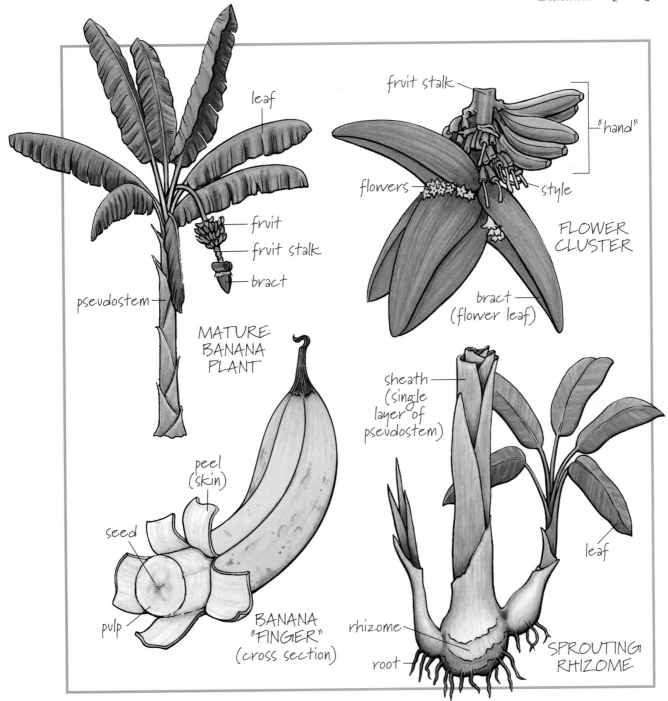

leaf

fruit stalk

"hand"

flowers

style

FLOWER
CLUSTER

fruit

fruit stalk

bract

bract
(flower leaf)

pseudostem

MATURE
BANANA
PLANT

sheath
(single
layer of
pseudostem)

peel
(skin)

leaf

seed

pulp

BANANA
"FINGER"
(cross section)

rhizome

root

SPROUTING
RHIZOME

Bananas are picked green. When ready for harvest, a farmhand cuts the stem with a sharp knife attached to a long pole. The heavy stem slowly bends down as it's being cut, coming to rest on the back of a second person, who carries the stem to either a cable conveyor system or a truck. The stems are taken to a processing area where workers run them through a water spray, cut them into clusters, and bathe the fruit again in a vat of water. When each small cluster has dried off, workers place a small label sticker on the

A picker carries a bunch of bananas. Workers place blue plastic bags on the bunches while still on the plant to protect the developing fruit.

fruit. Crews pack the bananas into cardboard boxes, load the fruit onto trucks or boxcars, and send the produce to a seaport.

Conveyor belts help dockworkers load the boxes of bananas into refrigerated ships. During the voyage, inspectors regulate the temperature of the ship to ensure the produce will be at the appropriate stage of ripeness upon arrival. Many wholesale banana buyers then put the fruit in special ripening rooms that recreate tropical conditions. This way, the bananas that consumers buy at the store are just yellow enough for appeal but green enough to stay fresh until they're sold.

Women wash bananas at a processing plant.

Big Business

Bananas are U.S. consumers' favorite fruit. We eat more than 28 pounds per person per year. Hawaii, the only U.S. source of the fruit, supplies 13 million pounds of bananas annually, only 1 percent of total consumption. Costa Rica, Ecuador, Honduras, Guatemala, and Colombia provide most of the rest. Bananas also grow in tropical Africa, Southeast Asia, and even Central Asia.

Eating Gold

Bananas can be mashed, fried, battered, stewed, or eaten just plain. While many North American banana eaters seem content to slice bananas on cereal, blend them into smoothies, or mash them up to feed babies, the rest of the world is more inventive. Mexicans add bananas to a stew that includes three kinds of meat, chickpeas, a range of vegetables, and massive amounts of garlic. Costa Ricans splurge on banana-lime ice

To Your Health!

In the A.D. 700s, Chinese physicians recommended dried banana rhizome for a number of troubles, including jaundice—a disease that turns the patient's skin yellow. Modern people know that the mild, sweet fruit is especially suited for soothing the tummy of anyone having trouble with digestion. Low in fat and high in fiber (which aids intestinal function) and carbohydrates (which provide energy), the banana is also a remedy for constipation.

A young banana seller waits for customers at a floating market in Thailand.

A food vendor in Thailand grills up a batch of bananas.

cream, and Puerto Ricans make a meat pie filled with plantains, beef, raisins, and capers (the bud of a Mediterranean shrub).

Baby plantains cooked in a floury cheese sauce are popular in Martinique. People on Antigua, another Caribbean island, bake bananas with rum and lime juice. Jamaicans prepare a rich drink of bananas, cream, vanilla, and sugar. Banana fritters made with sugar and corn flour are popular throughout the Caribbean and in Africa, too.

Tanzania, on Africa's southeastern coast, is banana country. Here people can enjoy a complete meal of bananas, starting with a meat-and-tomato-based cream of banana soup. Diners advance to a coconut, banana, and beef stew and finish with a banana-cream custard, all accompanied by banana wine. Just northeast of Tanzania, Kenyans favor bananas baked with peanuts. People throughout Africa eat banana chips, as do Hawaiians.

Indonesians wrap fish in banana leaves and steam the packages. In Kerala, a state in southern India, where dozens of banana varieties grow, cooks make fried banana chunks and mix bananas with hot spices and coconut. Bananas and yogurt are the basis of a spicy stew. Keralans serve some vegetarian meals on a banana leaf, called a *thali.*

Dig In!

PLÁTANOS FRITOS (FRIED PLANTAINS)
(4–6 SERVINGS)

4 semi-ripe plantains
canola oil or other cooking oil
dash of coarse salt
mayonnaise or ketchup

This variation on a Costa Rican dish is easy and tasty. You can find plantains, the bananas that must be cooked before eating, at a large natural-foods store, an ethnic market, or a supermarket. Firm, underripe bananas will also work in a pinch.

Peel and cut the plantains into 1- to 1½-inch segments. In a heavy skillet, heat enough canola oil to coat the bottom. Fry both sides of the plantains at medium heat, lightly browning the pieces. Remove them from the pan. Place the plantains between two plates and press down until the pieces are round and flat, somewhat like pancakes. Add a little more oil to the skillet if needed and refry the plantain slices on both sides until brown. Remove from the pan and drain on paper towels. Sprinkle the plantains with the salt and serve with a dollop of mayonnaise or ketchup. Eat quickly before they disappear.

Pineapples

[Ananas comosus]

Sometimes called the king of fruit because of its spiky crown, the pineapple has waxy leaves that retain moisture. The leaves' sharp edges also deter munching animals. One or two fruits grow from the center of the shrubby, two-to-three-foot plant.

A sweet, juicy, tropical delight, the pineapple is a native of Brazil and neighboring Paraguay. The Tupí-Guaraní Indians of the area cultivated the fruit thousands of years ago and carried the plant throughout the tropics of the South American continent. In ancient Peru, pineapples decorated pottery. The Carib Indians of the West Indies indicated welcome to friends by hanging pineapples above their dwelling places. They sent a somewhat different signal to their enemies—the Carib fortified their villages with spiky pineapple hedges.

A basket of fresh pineapple tempts shoppers at a French open-air market.

2 September 1741.... [W]e eat a pine apple, a most delicious mixture of a pomegranate, a melon, a quince, and most other fine fruits.

—William Stukeley

[26]

Native Hawaiians welcome Captain James Cook to their island.

In 1493 on the West Indian island of Guadeloupe, Carib people shared pineapple with Christopher Columbus and his crew, who became the first Europeans to sample the fruit. Spanish traders who followed Columbus to the Americas in the early 1500s named the fruit *piña*, or pine, because of its resemblance to a pinecone. The Spaniards brought pineapples, possibly from Peru, back home with them. King Ferdinand of Spain was probably the first European V.I.P. to taste a pineapple.

Around the same time, Portuguese colonists found pineapples growing in Brazil. By the mid-1500s, they had carried the fruit to their colonies in India and Africa, as well as home to Europe. Brazilian pineapples were most likely the first to reach England, which received the fruit in 1555.

Spanish traders also carried the pineapples to their Asian ports of call. By 1594 people in China and the Philippines were well acquainted with the plant. Pineapples were growing on the Indonesian island of Java by 1599. They were late to reach the Pacific Islands but probably arrived with the British explorer Captain James Cook. Cook traveled throughout the Pacific in 1773 and 1774 and reached the Hawaiian Islands in 1778.

A Rare Fruit

In all these tropical regions, the pineapple was an outdoor cultivated crop. In Europe, on the other hand, the fruit became a pet project of wealthy landowners equipped with skilled gardeners and heated greenhouses. In 1672 the first greenhouse-grown pineapple in England was presented to King Charles II. But eventually the Caribbean island of Barbados, not European greenhouses, supplied the English elite with the bulk of their pineapples. Because of its rarity, the pineapple swiftly became a symbol to wealthy English people of their own good fortune and hospitality. Ornamental stone pineapples adorned pillars, and artisans carved pineapples on dining-room doorways and lavish bedsteads.

Elsewhere in Europe, Louis XIV, France's monarch from 1643 to 1715, also received the first pineapple raised in his country. Alas, greedy Louis stalled further production by cutting his royal lip on the spiky skin of the fruit—he couldn't wait for it to be peeled properly. In the mid-1700s, his successor, Louis XV, ordered the construction of a greenhouse solely devoted to pineapples.

Even though the European upper crust enjoyed pineapples, the fruit was less familiar to the average American of the time. Well-off American colonists wishing to impress their dinner guests built elaborate displays of fruit, topped by a single pineapple. The fruit was so expensive and rare that some fruit sellers rented pineapples to the wealthy for their dinner parties. The final recipients may have paid the most, since they were allowed the extreme privilege of eating it! As in England, the pineapple was a favorite theme to stencil on walls or to weave into tablecloths.

The pineapple fruit, shown on this New England doorway (inset), is still a popular household decoration.

It's a Fact!

Before the arrival of the pineapple, sugarcane plantations were a major agricultural enterprise in Hawaii. From the 1850s to the early 1900s, immigrants came to the islands to work the huge plantations. Chinese and Japanese laborers were the first to arrive. A wave of Portuguese people came in the 1870s, and Filipinos, Koreans, and Puerto Ricans followed later. This large, skilled labor pool enabled the establishment of pineapple operations in Hawaii at the turn of the century.

Pineapples Go Hawaiian

In January 1813, a Spaniard named Don Francisco Marín may have planted the first pineapple in Hawaii, then an independent kingdom. Marín, an adviser to the Hawaiian king Kamehameha II, noted the event in his diary. The islanders called the plant *halakahiki,* meaning "screw pine from a foreign land," because the pineapple resembled a familiar local plant. By the mid-1800s, Hawaiians were shipping pineapples to California. But since pineapples are always picked ripe, much of the produce arrived spoiled. Eventually it became clear that the way to profit from pineapples was to can them.

The first person to set up a commercial pineapple plantation in Hawaii was a British man named Captain John Kidwell. Heavy U.S. tariffs (taxes) on fruit made life tough for Kidwell's new venture, which folded in 1898 after only six years of business. Ironically, that year Hawaii became a U.S. territory, and all tariffs were removed.

By 1901 an American, Jim Dole, had established the Hawaii Pineapple Company on the Hawaiian island of Oahu. Two years later, his cannery was up and running. At about the same time, another U.S. entrepreneur, Arthur Earnes, started his own pineapple business in Hawaii.

Business continued slowly and steadily until 1913 when Henry Ginaca invented a machine that revolutionized the canning

Workers at a Dole cannery trim bits of skin that the Ginaca machine missed on these pineapples.

business. The "Ginaca," as the device came to be called, removed the outer skin, the core, and both ends of the pineapple in one easy motion. The new machine eliminated much time-consuming hand labor. Before the invention of the Ginaca, the Hawaii Pineapple Company could process almost 1,900 cases of canned pineapple a year. With the Ginaca, the cannery was processing a whopping one million cases per year by 1918. Dole and Earnes were off and running, soon to become the giant global businesses Dole Corporation and Del Monte, rivals from the start.

By 1951 three-fourths of the world's pineapple came from Hawaii. During the 1970s, foreign competition knocked Hawaii's share to one-third of the world's supply. Del Monte closed its last U.S. canning plant in 1982, and Dole in 1992. These days all the canned pineapple that Dole and Del Monte sell comes from Thailand, the Philippines, or Kenya. Both companies still ship fresh Hawaiian pineapples, but only the Maui Pineapple Company supplies canned fruit from Hawaii. The Maui Pineapple Company also sends fresh whole and cut pineapple by air to selected U.S. markets.

Each of the flowers on this blooming plant will become a part of the pineapple fruit.

To Your Health!

Pineapples are easily digested because they contain the enzyme bromelain, which breaks down proteins in food. Pineapples also contain vitamin A (important for eye and skin health), vitamin C (which keeps tissues healthy), and minerals, the most significant of which is manganese. Manganese is important in building and maintaining bones.

Eyeing the Pine

If you take a close look at a pineapple, you'll see it has eyes, much like a potato. These eyes indicate where the tiny flowers of the plant once were. The pineapple itself grows from these flowers, which form a circle on the plant's central stalk. The blossoms develop into individual minifruits that fuse together with the stalk. Another circle of flowers opens above the first circle, and another above that until an entire pineapple forms. Some varieties produce seeds, but the type commonly grown for eating does not.

Pineapple Planting and Picking

Large-scale pineapple growing, such as in Hawaii, is highly automated and yet requires the hand labor of many people. The Maui Pineapple Company, the only business still canning Hawaiian pineapple, employs 1,200 full-time workers and hires another 600 during the peak harvest period.

Pineapple planting can start at any time of the year in Hawaii. After a tractor tills the ground, machines lay plastic mulch (protective covering for soil) in 100-foot-wide blocks in the fields. Mulch keeps weeds at a minimum, conserves moisture, and helps to maintain soil temperature. Workers punch holes in the mulch and hand plant crowns, the leafy shoots at the tops of previously harvested pineapples. The growing pineapples receive water from rainfall and by drip

PINEAPPLE
FLOWER
CLUSTER

leaf

flower
bud
(unopened)

stem

leaf

PINEAPPLE
FRUIT
(cross section)

core

fruitlet

crown

leaf

shell (skin)

pulp

stem

cut stem

MATURE
PINEAPPLE
PLANT

Using a trowel, a farmhand plants pineapple crowns in Hawaii.

It's a Fact!

Pineapples yield a variety of useful products. Pineapple sugar syrup is used in processed foods. The pineapple skin can be made into cattle feed. The base of the plant is a source of bromelain, an enzyme that digests protein. Bromelain reduces the substances that can cause swelling and pain in the joints. Bromelain pills help to relieve the pain of arthritis. Bromelain may also prevent blood clots and ease heart-related chest pains such as angina.

irrigation, which delivers water directly to the roots by means of thin plastic tubes placed along the ground. The plants need about 18 to 20 inches of water per year and warm, but not hot, temperatures.

In 18 months or so, the pineapple produces its first fruit. Some plants grow pineapples for two years, and some for three. Most Hawaiian pineapple planters use chemicals to force the plants to flower at regularly planned intervals. Pineapple plants bear fruit for three years—a single fruit the first year and two the second and third years. Then growers cut the old plants down and replant the field.

At harvesttime, a truck carrying a 54-foot conveyor belt enters the field. A group of 14 farmhands walks behind the belt, which stretches over 28 rows. The pickers select the ripe pineapples from two rows each, breaking the fruit from the stem with a twisting motion. Pineapples to be sold fresh are handled carefully. A specially trained crew places the fruit gently on the conveyor belt. Trucks take the pineapples to the packing center, where workers wash, inspect, size, and box them. The boxes go onto airplanes for fast delivery to mainland markets.

The bulk of pineapples, however, end up at the cannery. Pickers cut the crowns off the fruit right in the field, and they toss both crown and pineapple onto the conveyor belt. The crowns will be used later for planting. One truck can hold 10 tons of fruit and 1 ton of crowns.

Engineers are working to develop a pineapple-harvesting machine that can select and pick pineapples as well as people do.

Thai workers follow a harvesting truck through a field of ripe pineapples.

The owners of this Ecuadoran fruit stand prepare for a busy day of selling oranges, pineapples, and watermelons.

At the cannery, laborers clean and sort the pineapples and then run them through the Ginaca machine, which peels, trims, and cores the fruit. Slightly imperfect fruit goes to a crushing machine to be turned into juice or crushed pineapple. The high-quality pineapples go to a slicing machine and into cans.

Sixty-three percent of all imported fresh pineapples eaten in the United States come from Costa Rica. The Philippines supplies almost half of U.S. pineapple juice and canned pineapple imports. Thailand and Indonesia supply most of the rest.

Dig In!

PINEAPPLE SMOOTHIE
(1–2 SERVINGS)

¾ cup pineapple juice
1 cup crushed pineapple
½ cup vanilla yogurt

OPTIONAL:
   1 soft banana, peeled
   ½ cup berries or melon cubes, any kind
   ⅓ cup grape juice

Pineapple is the star here, but all the fruits in *Yes, We Have Bananas* can find a place in this recipe. Place all the ingredients in a blender. Blend until smooth, and then drink.

A Slice of Heaven

Everywhere in the world, people cut up pineapples and eat them fresh. On the Pacific islands of Samoa and Tahiti, a carved-out pineapple sometimes serves as a bowl for other fresh fruits. People of the tropics enjoy pineapple juice plain and add it to a wide range of drinks. In Puerto Rico, coconut milk and fresh pineapple are mixed together into a refreshing drink. Cubans bake pineapple with chicken, and on the Southeast Asian island of Borneo, people braise lamb with pineapple, coconut, and spices. The Chinese add pineapple chunks to stir-fry dishes. In the United States and Canada, some people bake ham studded with pineapple slices.

Grapes
[Vitis vinifera]

A source of table fruit, raisins, vinegars, and wines, grapes grow all over the world both as wild vines and as stock in well-tended vineyards. Ranging from "white" (pale green) to "black" (deep purple), grapes come in all colors and in hundreds of different varieties. Green and red table grapes are on sale in most supermarkets. The Black Corinth variety, originally from Greece, produces reddish black grapes that make fine, tiny raisins. The "blue-black" Concord grapes grown in New York State are decidedly purple. Another New York grape is the Catawba, a red table grape. Snack foods for our most ancient relatives, grapes originated in both hemispheres. Globally, however, the Eastern Hemisphere species *Vitis vinifera* dominates. *Vitis vinifera* probably grew many thousands of years ago in the Caspian Sea area of modern-day Iran. Researchers in the Zagros Mountains of northwestern Iran have found clay vessels containing grape residues dating back to roughly 5000 B.C. From its homeland, the vine spread both south and west.

Reddish purple Delaware grapes ripen on the vine.

The sweetest grapes hang highest.

—German proverb

This stone carving from Sumeria (modern-day Iraq) depicts a group of friends drinking wine together.

To ancient people, grapes were most important not as a table fruit, but as a source of wine. Unknown to early people, the alcohol in wine acted as a preservative and made the drink safer than water, which often swarmed with disease-causing bacteria. Wine drinkers, therefore, didn't fall ill as often as those who didn't drink wine. Wine came to be regarded as a healthy beverage to be drunk at meals and as an important part of social occasions, a treat to be shared with a group. The drink also became a valuable export item for many societies. The roads and waterways that carried trade goods, including wine, also allowed people to exchange customs and ideas. In this way, wine helped to spread the influence of major civilizations—such as those of the Greeks, the Egyptians, the Arabs, and the Romans—across Europe, northern Africa, and even into Asia. The Egyptians were importing wine from Palestine (modern-day Israel and the Jordan

Valley) in about 3150 B.C. Grapes were familiar to the Sumerians of ancient Iraq, and these people mentioned the fruits in the famous epic poem of Gilgamesh, written in about 3000 B.C. Greeks began planting grapes about 1700 B.C. Egyptian paintings from 1450 B.C. depict grape growing, harvesting, and wine making. The paintings show that growing grapes involved considerable hand labor—a situation that hasn't changed much even in modern vineyards.

The Chinese received grapes by the second century B.C. in trade exchanges along the Silk Road, a caravan route that stretched from China and India through the Middle East to Rome. For centuries goods flowed both ways along the Silk Road as the Chinese traded silk and spices for Middle Eastern foodstuffs, glass, and linen.

By the first century B.C., Greek sailors had probably carried vines to southwestern Europe and possibly to the Italian island of Sicily—all of which became parts of the Roman Empire (27 B.C.–A.D. 476). The Romans, like the Greeks, were avid grape growers and spread the practice throughout their wide domain. They delighted in sweet table grapes, stored the fruit through the winter in raisin form, and drank grape juice and wine. As their empire sprawled across more and more territory, the Romans established trade networks to carry goods—wine prominent among them—to the far-flung reaches of their lands.

It's a Fact!

As time went by, wine's social importance evolved into religious importance. In Europe there even sprang up cults that worshiped wine gods. These sects' ritual use of wine may have influenced other religious people, including Jews and early Christians.

Roman soldiers received rations of vinegar, which they considered a healthy drink.

To squeeze large amounts of grape juice, people put the grapes in a vat and trampled them until the fruit was completely crushed, as in this French drawing from the 1200s.

Under Roman rule, people in what would become Italy, Spain, Portugal, and France fell in love with grapes.

The fall of the Roman Empire in A.D. 476 did not mean the end of the grape. Even though people no longer answered to Rome, they were happy to grow the grapes the Romans had left behind. What's more, the increasingly powerful Christian church, which used wine as part of worship, was quickly spreading its influence throughout the continent. The church had a stake in preserving Europe's extensive grape plantings.

Grapes in Northern Europe

The story of the grapevine's establishment in northern Europe is cloudy. Wild vines grew there from the beginning. Grapes dislike extremes of humidity, heat, and cold. So as the climate fluctuated in northern Europe following the Ice Ages—that is, in the last 10,000 years—grapevines may have come and gone. But Swiss sites dating from 6000 B.C. to 3000 B.C. reveal archaeological evidence of grapes. The Romans probably introduced domesticated grapes to their territory on the island of Great Britain during their occupation of modern-day England and Wales starting in A.D. 43.

Not until 1086, however, did grapes appear in English records, when 38 English vineyards were recorded as taxable properties. Vineyards in such northern locales as the Baltic countries (Estonia, Latvia, and Lithuania), Belgium, the Netherlands, northern Germany, and northern France were well established by the twelfth century. By the 1700s, wealthy English people expected fresh clusters of grapes from their greenhouses at the dining table. So the family gardener filled special vases with water and placed them on racks in cooled "fruit rooms." The vases held long vine stems with bunches of grapes, which dangled until needed. The gardener changed the water in the vases daily to keep the grapes fresh as long as possible.

Grapes Go Global

Starting in the 1500s and continuing through the 1700s, European explorers traveled the world, bent on finding new lands and new riches. Wherever they established settlements, they brought *Vitis vinifera,* eventually spreading the vine to southern Africa and Australia as well as to the Americas. Spaniards carried grapevines into modern-day Mexico, establishing vineyards there in the 1520s. Spaniards also introduced the plant to their South American colonies of Chile and Argentina around 1560. The colonial grape ventures were so successful that in 1595 the king of Spain banned any further commercial plantings in the Americas, because locally grown Mexican grapes were driving down the prices of imported Spanish grape products.

Grapevines still flourish at Mission San Luis Obispo in California.

From Vine to Wine

Wine and vinegar were born well before recorded history. In ancient times, people crushed grapes and other fruits for their juice. Someone in the distant past probably left some mashed grapes sitting around in a clay pot or in an animal skin. A taster returning to the grapes must have decided the juice had possibilities.

The change from juice to wine happens because of a process called fermentation, which is caused by yeasts (a kind of one-celled organism) clinging to the skin of the grape. The yeasts change the sugar in the grape juice into alcohol.

If wine is exposed to air for a prolonged time, bacteria—another one-celled organism—will change the alcohol into acid. The wine will become vinegar.

Spanish priests, however, were not commercial growers and thus were not bound to obey the king's law. They planted grapevines at their missions (religious settlements) along the coast of California—which in those days included Mexico's Baja Peninsula—as a source of wine for church rituals. Father Juan Ugarte planted the first vine in Baja California in 1697, and mission vineyards spread northward from there.

By 1821 the Mexican War of Independence had cut California's ties to Spain and had removed the mission's Spanish backing. Soon the missions were forced to give up their vineyards and equipment to local businesspeople. In 1839 William Wolfskill became the first U.S. commercial farmer to grow and ship table grapes from his land near present-day Los Angeles.

Different Place, Different Grapes

Vitis vinifera did not grow wild in North America, but other species, comprising 40 varieties, did. In the 1600s and 1700s, European settlers in the Massachusetts area described the local grapes as having a "foxy" taste, a certain musky quality that they didn't like. Preferring the grapes from their homelands, colonists repeatedly attempted to grow the *Vitis vinifera* vines they brought with them, but each planting failed. Only grapes bred from native species such as Concord, Catawba, and Niagara grew successfully. **Hybrid** species from a mix of native grapes and *Vitis vinifera* also fared well.

The settlers blamed their grape failures on eastern North America's cold winter temperatures and year-round high humidity. These problems did, indeed, hamper the growth of finicky Old World grapes. The

It's a Fact!

In about A.D. 1000, well before the voyages of Christopher Columbus, Viking explorer Leif Eriksson sailed west from Iceland. He came upon a land filled with wild grapes, and he called the place Vinland. Historians think Vinland was on the east coast of North America somewhere between the modern-day Canadian province of Newfoundland and Labrador and the U.S. state of Massachusetts.

Prosperous French vineyard owners would face sudden ruin in the 1870s. The cause was the tiny phylloxera insect, which nearly wiped out Europe's grapes.

more certain culprit, however, was an aphid-like insect called phylloxera, so tiny that it escaped the notice of busy grape growers. Since the native East Coast grapes shared their homeland with the little bug, the vines had become resistant over time. But phylloxera could attack vulnerable *Vitis vinifera,* destroying the root system and quickly killing the plant.

By the 1870s, phylloxera had quietly invaded Europe, probably traveling on a botanical specimen of an American grape cutting. Soon the insect ate its way through France's finest vines. Millions of grapevines died before Europeans figured out that the pinprick-sized pest was to blame. Then New World grapes came to the rescue. European grape growers **grafted** their beloved *Vitis vinifera* onto tough, phylloxera-resistant rootstock from Massachusetts. The rescue took time and faced a few setbacks, but eventually the plan succeeded. To this day, classic European grape varieties grow on the roots of their American cousins.

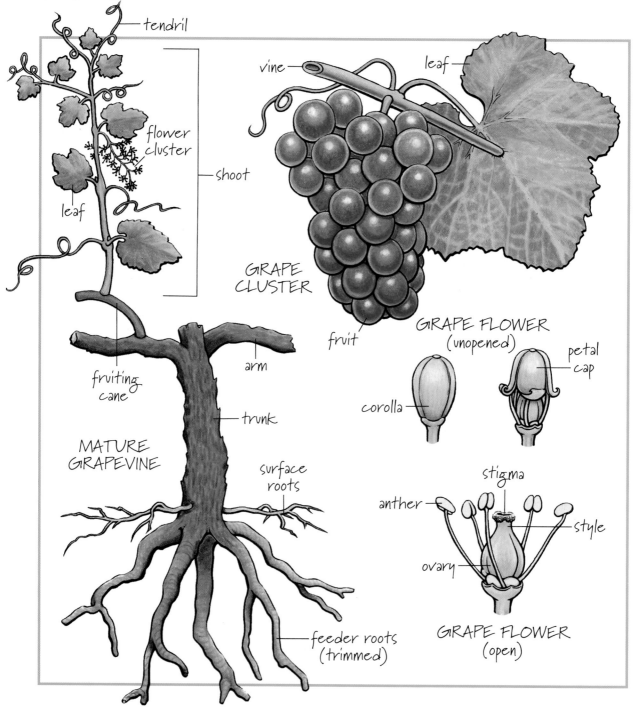

tendril

vine

leaf

flower cluster

shoot

leaf

GRAPE CLUSTER

fruit

GRAPE FLOWER (unopened)

petal cap

corolla

arm

fruiting cane

trunk

MATURE GRAPEVINE

surface roots

stigma

anther

style

ovary

GRAPE FLOWER (open)

feeder roots (trimmed)

Grape Growing and Harvesting

All grapes grow on vines. Most grapevines are planted from cuttings—parts cut from existing vines—that have grown in a greenhouse bed for at least a year. Sometimes a planter will graft a cutting from one vine onto another to form a new plant, which the grower then roots in the greenhouse.

In the springtime, when the vines are ready to plant outdoors, farmhands place each root in well-worked soil, about 6 to 8 feet apart. Because all vines need support to produce well, the grapes are planted directly

Workers plant new grapevines in Sonoma, California.

on a stake and a **trellis.** The grapes also need plenty of water. Many vineyards that can't rely on rainfall install irrigation systems, usually sprinklers or drip irrigation. The vines grow steadily for three or more years, attaching themselves to the trellises with thin growths called tendrils. Growers work their grape vines carefully, training them in the desired direction and pruning (trimming or cutting back) the plants regularly, usually twice a year. Pruning forces new growth and discourages crowding. Growers even prune out individual berries within a cluster of table grapes to give the remaining fruit enough room to plump up. Within five years, the vines can grow good grapes. They can produce well for another decade, then at lesser capacity for an additional 10 to 20 years. Some vines have been known to produce for 100 years or more.

A British farmworker picks grapes by hand.

A tractor picks green grapes to be crushed into juice.

Come harvesttime, some 60 to 100 days after flowering, pickers use special shears to hand cut clusters of table grapes from the vine. Often the pickers wrap the grapes in paper and pack them into wooden boxes right in the vineyard. Other growers deliver the grapes to packing houses, where rows of workers handle the packaging.

Machines frequently pick the grapes destined for wine or raisins. The grape-harvesting machine stands about 10 feet high so that it can straddle the vines. As the mechanism moves along the row, it shakes the vines and knocks the grapes onto a conveyor belt. The belt transports the fruits into a large tank in the adjacent row. A tractor, keeping pace with the harvester, pulls the tank. When the tank fills up, its load is dumped into a waiting truck, which brings the grapes to the winery for pressing.

Raisin' Raisins

Raisins have been around since the first grape dried up in the sun. A grape seeker probably tried the shriveled, dry version and found it tasty. Ancient peoples, including the Egyptians, became adept at drying grapes and other fruits in the sun. People might even have buried grapes under the hot desert sands to dry them. For thousands of years, raisin lovers used these simple methods to produce sweet snacks.

To Your Health!

Raisins are filled with fiber, potassium (which helps to maintain the body's fluid balance), vitamin A, and vitamin C. They are high in iron, which enables the body to use oxygen, and they provide fructose (fruit sugar) for good jolts of energy. Both grapes and raisins have a reputation for cleansing the intestines. The newest attraction for the grape is phenolics, chemical compounds that act as antioxidants. That is, they help eliminate toxins from the body. Phenolics also help lower levels of cholesterol, which can form an unhealthy buildup inside blood vessels.

Even though raisins have been around for ages, it took a massive heat wave in the 1870s to jump-start the California raisin business. The entire grape crop of the San Joaquin Valley turned to raisins. These days this area produces 95 percent of the U.S. raisin crop, most of it with hand labor. The world's leading exporter of raisins, however, is Turkey.

Most U.S. raisins are processed from a white table grape called the Thompson Seedless. The grapes can end up either as brown, sun-dried raisins or as golden raisins. Sun-dried raisins dry for two to three weeks (where else?) in the sun, on paper trays right out in the vineyard. They turn a dark, reddish brown. To make golden raisins, growers wash the grapes in warm water and place them on indoor wooden trays. Warm air

Raisins dry in the California sun. It takes four and a half pounds of grapes to make one pound of raisins.

blows on the grapes for 24 hours to dry them out. Then raisin makers apply a colorless gas called sulfur dioxide to preserve the gold color of the raisins. Golden raisins tend to cost more. If eaten uncooked, these raisins may have a sulfurlike taste.

Gobbling Grapes

California grows 90 percent of all the grapes produced in the United States—6 million tons. Washington State comes in a very dis-

Wine is a part of dinner for this French family.

tant second. All that fruit isn't enough for grape-greedy Americans, who average about 7 pounds of fresh grapes per year per person. So the United States imports close to 375,000 tons more from elsewhere in the world, including 300,000 tons from Chile.

Like many fruits, grapes are best enjoyed fresh as a snack or a light dessert. Even so, in North America, grapes sometimes pop up as an ingredient in tuna salad, or as a complement to baked salmon. Grapes are made into jelly and juice the world over.

In a region stretching from North Africa through Greece and the Middle East and into Central Asia, grape leaves are wrapped

Israeli fruit and vegetable sellers offer grapes to shoppers.

Dig In!

VERMICELLI AND RAISINS
(4–6 SERVINGS)

2 tablespoons vegetable oil

2 cups vermicelli pasta, broken into
   1-inch pieces

2 cups hot water

¾ teaspoon ground cardamom

¼ cup sugar

¾ cup raisins OR ¼ cup each raisins,
   chopped dates, and chopped walnuts

Raisins lend their sweetness to this light dessert from Kenya in West Africa. Heat the oil in a large frying pan over medium heat. Add the vermicelli and sauté until light brown. Slowly add the hot water, then stir in the remaining ingredients. Cover the pan and reduce the heat to low. Simmer, stirring occasionally, until all the water is absorbed and the vermicelli is tender—about 10 minutes.

around mixtures of rice, ground meat, and other ingredients. Diners in the countries of the Middle East often enjoy fresh grapes and melons together. People around the world eat raisins plain or put them into all manner of sweet treats. Crushed grape seeds yield a cooking oil.

In many countries, wine is an everyday part of meals or an ingredient for dishes both sweet and savory. And for special occasions, the finest wine with the most extraordinary meal is the way to celebrate with friends and family. People use wine and vinegar to flavor cooked dishes and salads, too.

Berries

[*Fragaria* — strawberries]
[*Vaccinium* — blueberries and
 cranberries]
[*Rubus* — raspberries]

Berries, like an old friend visiting from afar, arrive suddenly in the summer, stay briefly, and then disappear, leaving us wanting more. The category includes blackberries, boysenberries, gooseberries, elderberries, huckleberries, loganberries, and more. We're zeroing in on the strawberry but will also touch on blueberries, cranberries, and raspberries.

Strawberries

The strawberry grows low to the ground, sending out long **runners** that root and form new plants. Rich, green, trifoliate (three-part) leaves shade white, five-petaled flowers, which grow into the plump, red berries. Botanically, the strawberry is not even a true berry like the blueberry or the cranberry, both of which contain their seeds on the inside. If you look closely at a strawberry, you will see it is studded on the outside with tiny seeds.

Different berries, from top, counterclockwise: strawberries, blackberries, raspberries, red and black currants, green gooseberries, and blueberries

The fruits that I find in the woods are . . . strawberries, cranberries, hurtleberries, and grapes of diverse sorts.

—William Penn

The genus name of the European wood strawberry (above), *Fragaria vesca*, comes from the Latin word *fraga*, meaning "fragrant." European artists have often depicted the strawberry, as in this medieval French painting (right).

The European wood strawberry *(Fragaria vesca)*, a plant of northern climates, thrives under relatively cool conditions. The berry probably originated on the woodsy hillsides of northern Italy and France. Strawberry seeds have turned up in archaeological digs in Denmark, Britain, and Switzerland. Ancient people in these places ate the rich, sweet harvest every summer. Strawberry plants probably covered a large area where local people came in season to eat, right on the spot. The berries were probably too small and too fragile to transport.

Ancient Greeks and Egyptians didn't know about wild strawberries, although later Roman chroniclers mentioned the fruit. The first known mention of "domesticated" strawberries came in the A.D. 1200s, when a doctor from Alexandria, Egypt, described them. Gardeners didn't truly domesticate strawberries but simply transplanted wild plants into beds.

Herbalists of the 1500s pushed the strawberry and its leaves as a medicine. Strawberries crept into Shakespeare's plays in the early 1500s, and around that time, growers were likely selling the berries on the streets of London. But strawberries were not domesticated, even for the well-to-do, until well into that century.

American-Made Berries

Meanwhile, several thousand miles across the Atlantic Ocean in the Americas, two species of strawberry—*Fragaria virginiana* and *Fragaria chiloensis*—had long been growing, respectively, on the Atlantic coast of North America and on the Pacific coasts of North and South America. Native American peoples had been enjoying the fruits for ages. In 1535 the French explorer Jacques Cartier, on a voyage to find gold and to chart new territories, noted "vast patches of strawberries"— most likely *Fragaria virginiana*—along the St. Lawrence River in Canada. Roger Williams, founder of Rhode Island and a chronicler of local Indian life, in 1642 described how the Indians made strawberry bread. Certain northeastern tribes also dried strawberries for use in winter. English colonists grew the local strawberry and sent it back to Europe. European gardeners, hoping to improve their own strawberry species, tried to breed European plants with the Virginia berry. The plants would not **cross-pollinate,** although the American berry grew well by itself.

The Virginia berry's cousin *Fragaria chiloensis,* sometimes called the Chilean strawberry, bore large, pale-yellow fruits. Native Americans had cultivated the berry for some time. In 1712, while on duty in Chile to spy on Spanish fortifications, amateur botanist

Strewn Berries

Even though straw is customarily used as mulch on strawberry plants, straw probably did not give the berry its name. Strawberry comes from an Old English word something like *streow.* The word describes the plant's habit of strewing or scattering itself along the ground.

Captain Amédée-François Frézier decided to bring some strawberry plants home to France. But Frézier's selections did not produce sufficient pollen to provide many strawberries. Thus the plants bore fruit inconsistently and only with much struggle on the part of growers. In addition, most European gardeners found the Chilean berry tasteless and boring compared to the tiny, wild, European strawberry. But by the 1740s, people had planted *Fragaria chiloensis* next to its relation, *Fragaria virginiana*. The plants interbred,

Plastic mulch protects the soil and traps moisture for the young plants.

and the resulting hybrid produced large, red, tasty berries. This plant, called *Fragaria ananassa*, these days provides the majority of commercially produced strawberries on the world market.

In the 1850s, breeders developed plants that produced more fruit, and commercial strawberry cultivation took off. During the 1930s and 1940s, California strawberry growers introduced new varieties for commercial use. Work on more disease-resistant fruits continues to this day.

Growing Strawberries

The strawberry business is expensive and full of risks. Rain, wind, and excessive temperatures can easily damage the plants. Yet if all goes well during the growing season, producers make more money on strawberries than on any other fruit. Strawberries are raised on a large commercial scale in Poland, Japan, Spain, and Italy, as well as in the United States, the world's leading producer.

Commercial strawberries grow in raised beds about nine inches high. First, workers cover the tilled land with plastic. Then, to kill any disease-causing bacteria or insects, most commercial farms fumigate the soil with a chemical spray called methyl bromide. A highly toxic substance, methyl bromide depletes the ozone layer—a part of the earth's atmosphere that blocks harmful rays

Strawberry Workers

In the United States, migrant workers from Mexico come to California to plant, tend, pick, and often pack the strawberry crop. California's 20,000 strawberry workers pick more than 915 million pints of berries each year. Many are paid by the piece, so they must pick quickly to make as much money as they can. Others are paid by the hour.

Strawberry workers are negotiating with growers to establish adequate wages, benefits, and housing. In 1998 Swanton Berry Farms in California became the first strawberry grower to agree to better terms for its workers.

of the sun. The U.S. government will no longer allow the chemical after 2005, so many farmers are already seeking alternative chemicals.

After spraying, farmhands remove all the chemical-contaminated plastic and throw it away. Then the workers lay drip-irrigation systems along the rows and cover the fields with fresh plastic mulch. They punch holes in the plastic and hand plant young strawberries that were started from cuttings in nursery beds. The plants grow to a height of four or five inches.

When the plants are ready for harvest, they often yield continuously for many weeks. Pickers must bend low as they move through the fields, carefully selecting the ripe berries and leaving the rest to mature. Strawberries are fragile, so the fieldhands must take great care to handle them with as little damage as possible. Workers frequently pack the strawberries right in the field, placing the fruit into small, green boxes or baskets and then putting those containers into large, flat boxes. The berries are then shipped either to distributors or to stores.

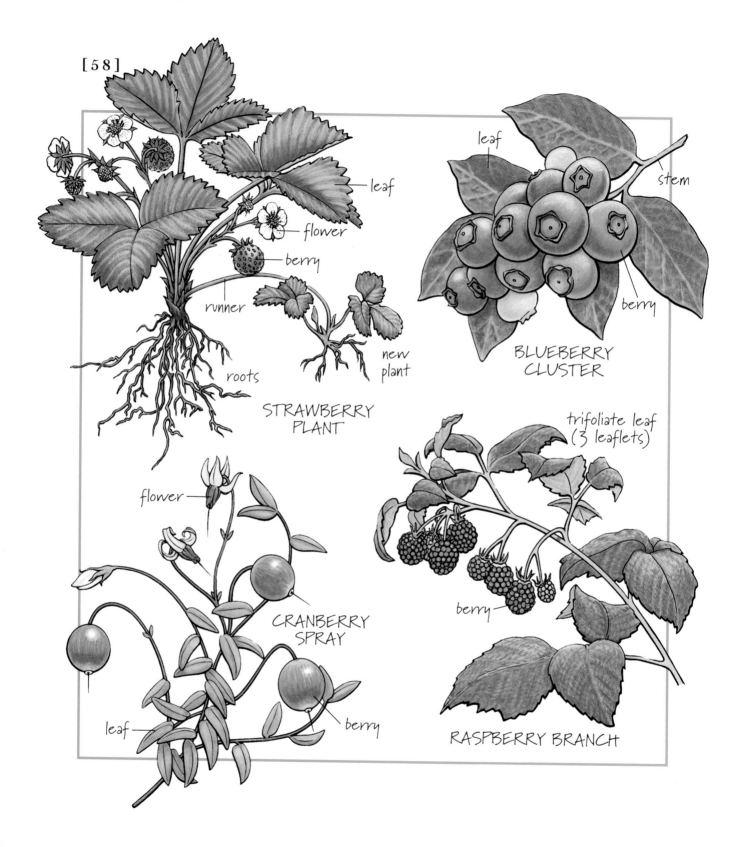

leaf

flower

berry

runner

roots

new plant

STRAWBERRY PLANT

leaf

stem

berry

BLUEBERRY CLUSTER

flower

CRANBERRY SPRAY

leaf

berry

trifoliate leaf (3 leaflets)

berry

RASPBERRY BRANCH

Strawberry Snacks

Each year the average American eats about four pounds of fresh and two pounds of frozen strawberries. The United States grows more than 814 tons of strawberries yearly. Purists may prefer to select the most perfect strawberries they can find and eat them plain or with a little sugar. But when Belgian chocolate makers dip strawberries into the finest, darkest, richest chocolate, simplicity goes out the window. And then there's strawberry shortcake, a typically American treat from the southern states. To make this dessert, people slice a flaky biscuit in half and slather both top and bottom with butter. Then they pile sugared strawberries between the two halves and on top. Fresh cream is then generously poured over the entire arrangement.

Of course, strawberries also go into jams, fillings for pies and tarts, and flavorings for ice cream. In Finland strawberries are the key ingredient in thick puddings called *kiisseli*. The Danes have their own strawberry pudding topped with slivered almonds.

Blueberries

The blueberry bush has small, oval-shaped leaves and delicate, white or pink, bell-shaped flowers. The blueberry loves cool temperatures and moist, acidic soils. This fruit is unusual in that much of its commercial produce comes from wild plants, usually

Strawberries taste good, and they're good for you—they're high in vitamin C.

the species *Vaccinium angustifolium*—also called the lowbush berry. Of the tall, domesticated highbush plants *Vaccinium corymbosum* is the most important species. Native to northern North America, the blueberry has also been grown successfully in several European countries.

We know little of the blueberry's early history. Native Americans picked and ate it on the spot and also dried it, as they did other fruits, for later consumption. Blueberries were also used as flavorings for stews and

To Your Health!

The blue in blueberries packs a healthy punch. The pigment in dark blue or dark red fruits, such as plums and blueberries, contains cancer-fighting substances called anthocyanins. These substances are also good for the skin. Anthocyanins promote healthy collagen, the protein that helps prevent facial wrinkles. In addition, wild blueberries have the highest levels of antioxidants among the fruits and vegetables we most commonly eat. Blueberries contain vitamins A and C, as well as the minerals potassium and magnesium.

soups. Indians who lived near Lake Huron made a pudding of cornmeal and ground blueberries called *sautauthig*. Certain Native Americans were said to admire the blueberry because the blossom end of the fruit forms a five-pointed star. Star berries were thought to be a gift directly from the Great Spirit to hungry children.

The Blueberry Business

Blueberries grow from underground rhizomes that thrive in sandy, heavily acidic soils. Commercial lowbush blueberry producers grow the wild shrubs where they find them—often on abandoned farmland where birds or other animals have scattered the seeds. Growers make the bushes produce more berries by controlling weeds, pruning, and fertilizing. They encourage new growth—which means new berries—by mowing or burning the bushes back every other year.

When the fruit is ripe, farmers can pick it either by hand or with mechanical harvesters. These machines strip the bushes of berries and send them by conveyor belt to a waiting truck. The berries go to processing plants for cleaning and, usually, freezing.

The most frequently grown commercial plants, though, are domesticated highbush blueberries. They need generous amounts of water and well-drained soil. Growers start highbush berries as cuttings in greenhouses. When the cuttings have grown roots and leaves, workers place the young plants outdoors in rows and then cover the beds with mulch to maintain moisture levels. Many growers bring beehives into the fields to ensure that busy honeybees fertilize the berry flowers. The bushes can produce fruit all summer. In British Columbia, which produces 95 percent of Canada's cultivated blueberries, fieldhands pick the berries two to four times a season, or every 10 to 14 days.

The United States produces more than 110 tons of blueberries annually. The state of New

Pickers dump blueberries into a cleaning machine.

Farmhands tend a new grove of highbush plants.

Jersey raises the country's biggest cultivated fresh blueberry crop. Michigan grows more berries, but two-thirds of the crop go for processing. Maine produces only wild blueberries, most of which are sold frozen. Canada raises close to 40 tons of the fruit each year. Poland, Lithuania, and the Netherlands are also significant blueberry-growing countries.

In addition to the United States, Chile, Sweden, Mexico, and Canada export frozen blueberries.

Blueberry Buffet

Blueberries with cream and blueberry muffins, pancakes, and pies mean summer to people of the northeastern United States and eastern Canada. Blueberry jam and ice cream turn up, too. In Finland blueberries are eaten fresh and made into large tarts. Finns dry blueberries for winter eating and favor a sweet blueberry soup, which they claim aids digestion.

While blueberries are not familiar to people all over the world, they are becoming popular in many countries, including Britain, Germany, and Italy. The people of Japan and France seem to be increasingly fond of the fruit—U.S. blueberry exports to these two countries are rising sharply.

Cranberries

Close relative to the blueberry, the cranberry grows from an evergreen vine with delicate, pink flowers and oval-shaped leaves. The plant acknowledged as the "true" cranberry, *Vaccinium macrocarpon*, originated in North America. These cranberries originally grew wild in sandy marshes in present-day Massachusetts, Rhode Island, and Wisconsin. A different cranberry, *Vaccinium ocycoccus*, grows in North America, Europe, and northern Asia.

Different groups of Native Americans gave the cranberry various names, including *sassamanesh*, *ibimi*, and *atoqua*. Native Americans ground or mashed fresh cranberries. Indians of eastern North America mixed dried berries with processed wild game to make pemmican, a winter survival food. They also prepared a sweet sauce with cranberries and maple syrup. The rich red of the berry's juice made a dye for blankets.

It's a Fact!

Because the blossoms of the cranberry plant resembled the head and beak of a tiny crane, a large bird familiar to European settlers in North America, they called it craneberry. Eventually the word lost its *e* to become cranberry.

A bog blushes pink with cranberry blossoms. At the end of the growing season, farmers flood the bog to help them harvest the fruit *(inset)*.

Because the fruit lasts a long time without spoiling, cranberries were one of the first foods to be shipped to Britain from the American colonies in the early 1700s. At about the same time, cranberries provided doses of vitamin C to American sailors, helping to ward off the disease scurvy. Gathered wild for many years, cranberries were first cultivated commercially in Massachusetts in 1816 and in Wisconsin around 1860.

Soggy, Boggy Growing

The cranberry grows in moist, low-lying areas. To prepare a commercial cranberry bog, growers carefully level the soil and cover their land with 3 or 4 inches of sand. Then, in the springtime, cranberry growers plant more than one ton of vines per acre, either by hand or by scattering the vines on the sandy ground and driving a roller over them to press them into the soil. In early fall, when the berries are ready to harvest, many farmers flood their bogs with water 6 to 12 inches deep. Mechanical harvesters then remove the berries from the swamped vines. The fruits float to the surface, where berry pickers haul them in with wooden frames. Conveyor belts on dry land carry the berries to trucks, which take them to processing plants.

Commercial cranberries are grown in five states: Massachusetts, Wisconsin, New Jersey, Oregon, and Washington. Americans eat 400 million pounds of cranberries each year—80 million in the week of Thanksgiving alone! Chile and Canada also grow cranberries.

Cooked with water and sweetener, cranberries make a great sauce. They also go into muffins and breads and provide juice. In Finland native cranberries are the basis of several alcoholic drinks called liqueurs.

Workers use a wooden frame to round up the floating berries.

Dig In!

CRANBERRY NUT BREAD
(1 LOAF)

1 cup cranberries, fresh or frozen
¾ cup orange juice
2 cups flour
1½ teaspoons baking powder
1 teaspoon salt
½ teaspoon baking soda
1 egg, well beaten
2 tablespoons cooking oil
1 tablespoon grated orange peel
½ cup chopped walnuts

Preheat the oven to 350°. Grease and lightly flour a 9x5x3-inch loaf pan. Put the cranberries in a blender with the orange juice. Blend very briefly, until the berries are chopped, then set the mixture aside. In a large bowl, mix together the dry ingredients. In a smaller bowl, mix together the egg, the cranberry-juice mixture, the oil, and the orange peel. Add the contents of the smaller bowl to the larger bowl and fold together until just mixed. Scatter the nuts over the batter and stir briefly to mix. Spoon the batter into the loaf pan and bake 60 minutes or until a toothpick inserted in the middle of the loaf comes out clean. Remove the bread from the oven and cool 15 minutes. Remove the loaf from the pan, cool it a little longer, and then slice and eat.

This cluster of raspberries is ready to pick.

Raspberries

The raspberry is a woody plant, growing from a shallow, yet often spread-out, root system. The raspberry and its family members are always a challenge to hungry pickers. Thorns or prickles protect the plant up and down the length of its stems, called canes. Raspberries may be purple, black, or even yellow, as well as the familiar red. Like strawberries, raspberries are not true berries. They are a cluster of small fruitlets, each of which holds a seed. The cluster grows around an inedible white core that stays on the bush when the fruit is picked. Two kinds of raspberries predominate in the world: *Rubus idaeus,* a European species; and *Rubus strigosus,* native to North America.

Some 200 species of raspberry grow in east Asia, so it seems likely that *Rubus idaeus* originated there thousands of years ago, probably in modern-day Turkey. In fact, in 65 B.C., the Roman general Pompey brought home raspberries picked on the slopes of Mount Ida, near the ancient city of Troy in present-day Turkey.

For centuries the raspberry remained a wild fruit, gathered and enjoyed seasonally. Perhaps because raspberries grew in such abundance in cooler climates, people had more than enough to eat without bothering to cultivate the crop. The fruit's planting was handled by birds, who ate the berries and then scattered the undigested seeds far and wide in their droppings.

In the 1600s in England and France (somewhat earlier in Germany), people began to plant raspberries in their gardens and to select certain plants for desirable traits, thereby developing new varieties. Colonists settling the Americas in the late 1600s and early 1700s found native raspberries growing wild but introduced their familiar European types anyway. To this day, in rural areas, one can find patches of European varieties that, with the help of birds, have fled the garden to take up life as "wild" raspberries.

Grow 'Em, Then Eat 'Em

To plant a raspberry patch, growers start by cutting suckers—that is, new canes that sprout from the roots of older plants. The suckers grow for a year in greenhouse beds before farmers (or, frequently, home gardeners) transplant them outdoors. They often stake the plants or provide wire trellises for additional support. After a year or two of growth, raspberry canes bear flowers in late spring or early summer, produce the fruit, and then die. Growers cut back the canes so that new stems will grow. Too many new canes, however, mean lesser-quality berries, so growers prune the plants, leaving only a few stems on each.

Known for their delicious flavor in pies, jams, sorbets, tarts, cookies, or just plain, raspberries are also crushed for wine and vinegar. Raspberry vinegar is tasty in salad dressings, and some people say it's helpful as a gargle for sore throats.

A grower inspects his raspberry bushes.

Boxes of red and yellow raspberries wait for buyers at a Finnish market stall.

Melons

[*Citrullus vulgaris*—watermelons]
[*Cucumis melo*—muskmelons]

Cousins to the cucumber and the squash, melons grow on long, trailing vines. Each plant's yellow blossoms attract bees for pollination. The spreading green leaves provide shade during the day, keeping the fruit from burning in the sun. Melons are divided into two very broad groups—muskmelons and watermelons.

The seeds of muskmelons are centrally gathered in a cavity. The fruits can have rough or smooth skin. Most, but not all, muskmelons have raised ribs and heavy netting (rough, netlike patterns) on their rinds. The category includes Persian melons with salmon-colored flesh; yellow-skinned Casaba melons, named for Kasaba, Turkey; and crenshaw melons. The melons that North Americans call cantaloupes are a variety of muskmelon, too, but they aren't really cantaloupes. True cantaloupes, grown in Europe, have wartlike growths on their hard, green skin. Winter melons are smooth-skinned muskmelons, and they include the green-fleshed variety called honeydew.

A variety of tasty muskmelons surrounds half a sweet, juicy, red watermelon.

*...Stumbling on melons,
as I pass,
Insnar'd with flowers,
I fall on grass.*

—Andrew Marvell

Seedless watermelon

It's a Fact!

Spiky, orange bitter melons are not melons at all but are closely related to the cucumber. Many Asian people eat the bitter melon as a vegetable, usually cooked and often pickled.

Watermelons are usually smooth skinned with seeds scattered throughout the flesh. Some botanists insist that the watermelon is not a melon at all but more truly a sweet, pink-fleshed cucumber. They back up their claim with the fact that muskmelons easily cross-pollinate with one another to form new hybrids, but watermelons won't mix with other melons.

Watermelons are round or oblong, and some varieties have yellow flesh instead of pink. So-called seedless watermelons do have a few white seeds, but nothing like the seed count required for a genuine summer seed-spitting contest. Although there are more than 500 different varieties of watermelon worldwide, only a handful are grown commercially, some just in certain regions. If you ask for watermelon, you might get a slice of Jubilee, Sugar Baby, Desert King, Peacock, or Huck Finn.

Melons through the Millennia

Muskmelons probably originated in the Middle East, most likely in modern-day Iran. The Sumerians were growing melons as early as about 3000 B.C. They mention the fruits in the Gilgamesh epic. Egyptian tomb paintings dating from about 2400 B.C. depict melons. Watermelons originated somewhere in Africa, where farmers cultivated them as early as 2000 B.C. The Bible frequently mentions melons—the chapter of Exodus describes how the ancient Hebrews missed the fruit during their wanderings in the desert.

Middle Eastern traders brought melons to Greece and to China around the third century B.C. By the third century A.D., the Romans were probably importing melons from the Central Asian country of Armenia rather than growing their own.

With the collapse of the Roman Empire in A.D. 476, melon imports from Asia ceased. Melons were a distant memory until the Moors conquered southern Spain in the eighth century, bringing their fruits and vegetables with them. By the early 1500s, melons again grew regularly in formerly Roman settlements in southern France and Italy.

According to legend, the Sumerian hero Gilgamesh was a melon fan.

The Sandia Mountains take their name from the area's watermelon-pink sunsets.

Melons Make Their Move

At about the same time, Spaniards brought melons to their colonies in South America and Mexico. Exploring north of modern-day Mexico in the 1540s, a group of Spaniards arrived just at sunset in the mountains east of the Rio Grande. The pink glow on the mountains reminded the explorers of the flesh of a watermelon, or *sandía*. These days the Sandia Mountains form a backdrop for the city of Albuquerque in New Mexico.

Watermelons may have arrived in North America with African slaves in the early 1600s, and Indians along the Rio Grande were growing the fruit by the late 1600s. The Hopi of present-day Arizona and New Mexico nicknamed watermelons "horse pumpkins," because they thought a fresh watermelon smelled like a sweating horse. Early watermelon varieties were good keepers. The Navajo of Arizona hung them in slings for winter storage. Many groups dried and ate watermelon seeds. A coating of crushed watermelon seeds still keeps piki bread—a blue cornbread invented by the Hopi Indians and made by various Indians of the Southwest—from sticking to the stone slab on which it's prepared.

Indians of the Southwest grew muskmelons but did not prize them as highly as watermelons. People often peeled muskmelons, removed the seeds, and hung up the flesh to dry for a day. Then they cut the fruit into long strips and twisted the strips into spirals, which they bundled and hung up to store.

Growing Melons

Most commercially grown melons start life in greenhouses. In the spring, farmworkers plant the 3-inch seedlings in rows—8 to 12 feet apart for watermelons, closer together for smaller melons—in raised beds of sandy soil. Melon vines grow quickly, as much as 8 feet a month. Some growers place beehives in the field to ensure pollination of the flowers. Within 60 days of planting, the fruit appears. After another 30 days, it is ready to harvest.

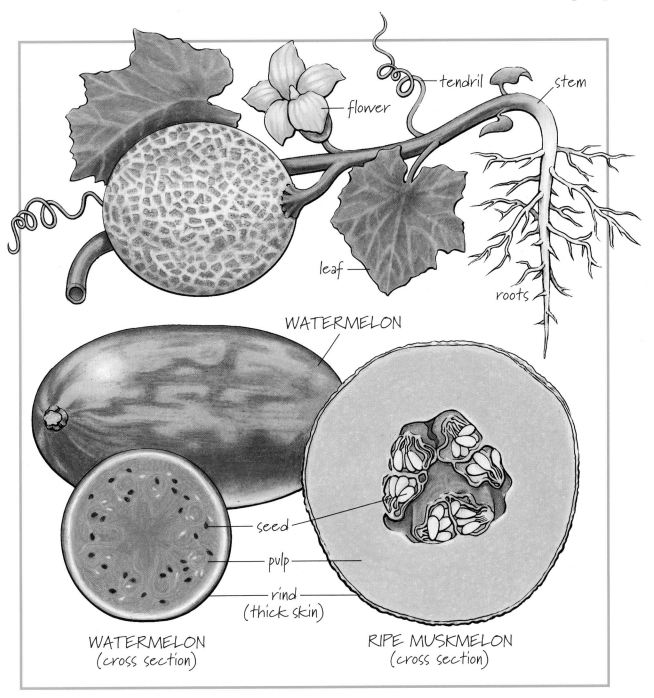

flower

tendril

stem

leaf

roots

WATERMELON

seed

pulp

rind
(thick skin)

WATERMELON
(cross section)

RIPE MUSKMELON
(cross section)

These yellow blossoms in South Africa's Kalahari Desert will grow into delicious melons.

To Your Health!

Containing 92 percent water and only about 5 percent sugar, melons are refreshing and cooling, a special favorite of desert dwellers. Melons also have some vitamin C and vitamin A. Competitive runners grab melon chunks in the middle of a race for a quick dose of potassium, which helps prevent leg cramps.

The fruit closest to the root matures earliest. Melons growing at the other end of the vine will take longer to ripen.

Melons must be fully ripe when picked. They look hefty and strong, but they're very fragile. That's why melons are usually hand harvested. Fieldhands carry the heavy fruit to trucks that bring the crop to packing sheds. Some growers pack melons right in the field to avoid extra damage to the produce.

Many Melons

Watermelon is the most frequently consumed melon in the world. China produces a staggering 38 billion pounds of it each year, more than nine times what the United States grows. The Chinese delight in the inexpensive, sweet watermelon. They eat more watermelon than any other fruit and grow it in nearly every province. Turkey and Iran are a distant second and third to China in world watermelon production. Florida and Georgia are the two biggest U.S. growers, each providing 18 percent of the total watermelon crop. But California grows the most U.S. melons overall, and half of the crop is American cantaloupe.

All this melon has to find ready customers, of course. Among the world's melon eaters, the Turks are tops—on average the people of Turkey annually consume an astonishing 223 pounds of melon per person. The Israelis take second place with 179 pounds. The average American eats only about 30 pounds of melon per year: 16 pounds of watermelon,

There's nothing like a big slice of watermelon on a hot day.

12 of cantaloupe, and 2 of honeydew. Even so, to have a supply during the winter and early spring, the United States imports more melons than any other country.

Munching Melons

People eat most melons fresh, in chunks or slices. In many parts of Asia, roasted watermelon seeds are a treat, and people might use ground seeds to make bread. Russians make drinks from fermented watermelon juice.

Chinese cooks combine ham, mushrooms, winter melon, and chicken broth for melon soup, which they sometimes serve in the carved-out melon itself. The Chinese also carve out watermelons and fill them with an array of exotic fruits. Watermelon-rind pickles are a Greek specialty that turned up in Charleston, South Carolina, years ago and have since become a southern tradition.

A Chinese watermelon seller is ready to greet the day's customers.

Dig In!

MELON-BERRY FRUIT CUP
(6 SERVINGS)

1 cantaloupe, cut into balls or chunks
½ honeydew, cut into balls or chunks
1 cup watermelon balls or chunks
1 cup blueberries
1 cup strawberries, halved
½ cup raspberries
1 cup green grapes, halved
½ to 1 cup orange juice, to taste
6 sprigs fresh mint, chopped

Wash all the fruit well. To prepare
melon balls, cut the muskmelons in half
and scoop out the seeds, or cut a large
chunk of watermelon. Using a melon
baller, scoop out the flesh using a
twisting motion. Don't scoop out portions
of rind, though—stick to the soft,
sweet part of the melon. If you don't

have a melon baller, then be content with chunks. Cut the melon into slices about 1
inch thick, pare off the rind (carefully—the melon is slippery), and slice the flesh
into chunks about 1 inch square.

   Combine all the fruit in a large bowl. Pour the orange juice over the fruit and
toss until all the pieces are coated with juice. Chill. Serve in individual dishes and
top each fruit cup with the chopped mint.

Glossary

berry: Any fruit that consists of a single, enlarged ovary (the part of a flower that becomes a fruit) with many seeds embedded in its flesh. Alternately, any small, seedy fruit.

cross-pollinate: To reproduce by fertilizing the flowers of neighboring plants.

domestication: Taming animals or adapting plants so they can safely live with or be eaten by humans.

graft: To unite two plants by placing a stem or bud of one into a cut in the other, then allowing the two parts to grow together.

herb: A plant with a soft, rather than a woody, stem.

hybrid: The offspring of a pair of plants or animals of different varieties, species, or genera.

photosynthesis: The chemical process by which green plants make energy-producing carbohydrates. The process involves the reaction of sunlight to carbon dioxide, water, and nutrients within plant tissues.

rhizome: A rootlike, underground stem.

runner: A stem that grows along the ground and forms new plants at one or more points along its length.

trellis: A framework of crossed wooden strips used to support climbing plants.

tropics: The hot, wet zone around the earth's equator between the Tropic of Cancer and the Tropic of Capricorn.

Further Reading

Burns, Diane L. *Cranberries: Fruit of the Bogs*. Minneapolis: Carolrhoda Books, Inc., 1994.

Busenberg, Bonnie. *Vanilla, Chocolate, & Strawberry: The Story of Your Favorite Flavors*. Minneapolis: Lerner Publications Company, 1994.

Fitzsimons, Cecilia. *Fruit*. Englewood Cliffs, NJ: Silver Burdett, 1996.

Kite, L. Patricia. *Gardening Wizardry for Kids*. Hauppauge, NY: Barron's Educational Series, Inc., 1995.

Nottridge, Rhoda. *Vitamins*. Minneapolis: Carolrhoda Books, Inc., 1993.

Overbeck, Cynthia. *How Seeds Travel*. Minneapolis: Lerner Publications Company, 1982.

Root, Waverly. *Food*. New York: Simon & Schuster, 1980.

Trager, James. *The Food Chronology*. New York: Henry Holt and Company, 1995.

Vendors at a Mexican fruit stand advertise fresh strawberries with cream.

Index

About the Author

Meredith Sayles Hughes has been writing about food since the mid-1970s, when she and her husband, Tom Hughes, founded The Potato Museum in Brussels, Belgium. She has worked on two major exhibitions about food, one for the Smithsonian and one for the National Museum of Science and Technology in Ottawa, Ontario. Author of several articles on food history, Meredith has collaborated with Tom Hughes on a range of food-related programs, lectures, workshops, and teacher-training sessions, as well as *The Great Potato Book*. The Hugheses do exhibits and programs as The FOOD Museum in Albuquerque, New Mexico, where they live with their son, Gulliver.

Acknowledgments

For photographs and artwork: Steve Brosnahan, p. 5; Tennessee State Museum Collection, detail of a painting by Carlyl Urello, p. 7; Holt Studios/Inga Spence, pp. 11, 47 (top), 48, 56; Air-India Library, p. 13; © SuperStock, pp. 14, 59, 72; North Wind Picture Archive, p. 15; © Karlene Schwartz, p. 16; Library of Congress, pp. (LC–D4–39636) 17, 28, (LC–D4–39463) 29 (inset); Hulton Deutsch/Corbis, p. 18; AP/Wide World Photos, p. 19; Holt Studios/Nigel Cattlin, pp. 20, 35, 55; © Inga Spence/Visuals Unlimited, pp. 22 (top), 57; © Robert E. Daemmrich/Tony Stone Images, p. 22 (bottom); © Mervyn Rees/Tony Stone Images, p. 23; Christine Osborne Pictures/Middle Eastern Pictures, pp. 24, 50 (bottom), 70 (bottom); © September 8th Stock, Walt/Louiseann Pietrowicz, pp. 25, 37, 65, 69, 76; © Corrine Humphrey/Visuals Unlimited, pp. 27, 70 (top); © Sylvan H. Wittwer/Visuals Unlimited, p. 29; Corbis/Bettmann, p. 31; © David Sieren/Visuals Unlimited, p. 32; © Greg Vaughn/TOM STACK & ASSOCIATES, p. 34; © Robert Fried, pp. 36, 50 (top), 67 (bottom), 78; © Bill Banaszewski/Visuals Unlimited, p. 39; E. T. Archive, pp. (Baghdad Museum) 40, (Biblioteca Estense Modena) 42, (Archaeological Museum Aleppo) 71; © Shirley Jordan, p. 43; Library of Decorative Arts, Paris, France/Explorer, Paris/SuperStock, p. 45; Holt Studios/Jean Hall, p. 47 (bottom); © Link/Visuals Unlimited, p. 49; Robert L. and Diane Wolfe, p. 51; © Maximilian Stock, Ltd./AGStock USA, p. 53; © David S. Addison/Visuals Unlimited, p. 54 (top); Paris et ses Historiens aux XIV et XV Sicles, 1867, p. 54 (bottom); © Richard L. Carlton/Visuals Unlimited, p. 60; © Jeff Greenberg/Photo Researchers, p. 61 (top); Holt Studios/Willem Harinck, pp. 61 (bottom), 64; © Cheryl Walsh Bellville, p. 62; © John D. Cunningham/Visuals Unlimited, p. 63; © Valorie Hodgson/Visuals Unlimited, p. 63 (inset); © D. Cavagnaro/Visuals Unlimited, p. 66; © Matthew McVay/Tony Stone Images, p. 67 (top); © K. Wanecek/OKAPIA/Photo Researchers, p. 74; © Don Smetzer/Tony Stone Images, p. 75 (top); © Sophie Dauwe/Robert Fried Photography, p. 75 (bottom). Sidebar and back cover art by John Erste. All other artwork by Laura Westlund. Cover photo by Steve Foley.

For quoted material: p. 4, M. F. K. Fisher, *The Art of Eating* (New York: Macmillan Reference, 1990); p. 10, as quoted by Alex Abella, *The Total Banana* (New York: Harcourt Brace Jovanovich, 1979); p. 26, as quoted by Brigid Allen, ed., *Food: An Oxford Anthology* (Oxford University Press, 1994); p. 38, March Egerton, *Since Eve Ate Apples: Quotations on Feasting, Fasting, and Food—from the Beginning* (Portland: Tsunami Press, 1994); p. 52, from a 1683 letter to the Committee of the Free Society of Traders, as quoted by Stephen Wilhelm and James Sagen, *A History of the Strawberry* (University of California Press: Berkeley,1974); p. 68, from "The Garden," as cited by Alice Mary Smith, ed., in *Oxford Dictionary of Quotations* (London: Oxford University Press, 1941).

For recipes (some slightly adapted for kids): p. 25, courtesy of Dylana Jenson; pp. 37, 65, 76, Meredith Sayles Hughes; p. 51, Constance Nabwire and Bertha Vining Montgomery, *Cooking the African Way* (Minneapolis: Lerner Publications Company, 1988).